CSS Programming for Beginners

How to Learn CSS in Less Than One Week. The Ultimate Step-by-Step Complete Course from Novice to Advance Programmer

William Brown

Table of contents

Introduction

We begin the book because we were hoping you could become a potential technology superstar; we hope to Get Coding to teach you how to code and demonstrate how much fun and exciting it can be. Coding is one of the most valuable abilities that young people can acquire, and there's never been a greater opportunity to experience it.

This book will show you how to code using the two most important programming languages, CSS and HTML, to create professional-looking websites. A machine may be programmed to do virtually any task, although it must first be programmed. The computer's program must be written in computer-friendly languages. Learning to code computer programming is what Coding is all about.

The two most commonly used programming languages for developing website in the world are HTML and CSS. Web developers use them to create blogs, games and web-based applications that we use and see daily. This book will show how to use these two programming languages to compose coda and create a program. This book teaches you practical coding skills that you will apply to every computer project.

This book is divided into six parts, each of which includes a mission to teach you HTML and CSS coding skills. It's up to you to make your way through the chapters and finish the missions with your abilities.

Chapter-1: CSS: An Overview

Cascading Style Sheets is the full form of CSS, and it is in charge of styling and rendering web material more presentable. Cascading Style Sheets (CSS) tell browsers how to view HTML tags in different ways. These style standards override the browser's default HTML tag layout laws. The style sheets are cascading because they will have several competing rules applied to a single tag, but the rules that are more clearly focused would overshadow the rules that are less directly targeted. CSS allows you to add designs to your web pages and modify them. The great thing about using this style function is that it is independent of how web pages are created using HTML.

The padding around table cells and the thickness and color of a table's border, photographs, and all other artifacts can all be described using CSS. CSS gives Web designers more precise power about the look of Web pages than HTML. Cascading design sheets are used for the majority of modern websites for this purpose.

1.1 HTML and CSS are two different languages.

The primary distinction between Hypertext Markup Language and Cascading Style Sheets is that the former is mostly popular for providing a structural way of the landscape of the web page. At the same time, the latter is intended to offer effective color coding and styling techniques. It is used to monitor the structure of several web pages at the same time. CSS files are used to contain all of the external stylesheets.

1.2 What is the purpose of CSS?

- Easy to maintain: To make a global update, merely adjust the style, and the other web pages' other elements would automatically improve.

- CSS saves time: You have to compose the script once, and you can reuse the same sheet as many times as you want.

- Having the better native front-end styles: CSS has a considerably greater number of attributes and lists than HTML. Consequently, the HTML page would have a lighter appearance and sound compared to normal HTML attributes.

- Provide Search Engines with a feature: CSS is a really basic and quick style sheet. It ensures that search engines don't have to do any effort to understand the text.

- Efficient and systematic cache storing: With the aid of an offline cache function, CSS may store web apps locally.

1.3 CSS Characteristics

One of CSS's key features is style guidelines, which are interpreted by the browser and applied to various elements in the code. The below are some of the major characteristics:

1.4 Compatibility

CSS allows users to remain stress-free when working on older language variants since it is backward compatible. As a result, though CSS programs are written in an outdated version of the programming language and the authors add modern modifications, CSS will be adopted and applied with such improvements. As a result, the modifications identified with CSS's predecessor do not need to be removed, and a developer may successfully upgrade the existing code.

1.5 Domain for E-Commerce

CSS has performed a significant part in the E-Commerce industry. In the E-Commerce sector, there are various industries, and CSS has aided the application systems styling and look-views that are used for small to large scale industries. CSS styling may be used to connect to an e-commerce website directly. Additionally, various add-ins and library files can be edited and upgraded by CSS libraries and used when developing web apps. CSS's source codes can be applied in the HTML system to create an e-commerce web portal from the ground up.

1.6 Upkeep of the website

Another popular explanation for the importance of CSS is that it allows you to express yourself creatively. When it comes to website upkeep, CSS is extremely necessary. It allows website upkeep a lot simpler. The CSS file gives the website a more portable look and feels, allowing it to be changed more easily. It also allows HTML formatting and data feature alteration more straightforward. As a result, website management becomes more convenient from the standpoint of growth.

1.7 The Influence of Social Media

The use of CSS in HTML systems is now being introduced into the creation of social networking websites. Facebook implementations may be linked to the relevant systems directly. The HTML client library files can be used to create an application using CSS stylings that can run with various extensions. These social media-based sites can be linked to applications and used to create a few enhancements from the viewpoint of the end consumer. As a result, CSS styling and upgrading the user interface is simplified, which significantly affects social networking sites.

1.8 User Interface and Web-based Online Community

According to the existing norm, CSS may be applied in a variety of ways to build any web-based website or online group. Different style sheet implementations are available in CSS, and they can be conveniently applied here. The style of one's online group can be created using CSS. There are also various add-ons available, which can be implemented using CSS frameworks to develop the web-based community's look and feel.

1.9 Convenient Accessibility

CSS apps have even better options in terms of accessibility, allowing developers to update the user interface to meet market needs. It also enables various users, such as speaking browsers and PDAs, to make web pages with ease. When it comes to changing the look and sound of a web page from the end-user and company viewpoint, this has a far bigger effect.

1.10 Handling Image Files

Where it comes to image processing, CSS includes the styling library, which aids in the output of images and XML to the viewer.

It was initially challenging to redesign and style the original picture. However, utilizing CSS folders, output images can now be received in various formats such as jpeg, png, and gif, which can then be changed to the desired styling formats. This functionality often allows you to manipulate various picture styles and construct thumbnails, watermarks, and image cropping, among other things.

1.11 Handling Dynamic Website Templates

CSS in the HTML format can be used to build though manage dynamic website templates, and it mostly aids in the addition and modification of web pages and components on the webserver and sites. It is simpler to manage dynamically assigned items by applying CSS extensions to the concerned HTML pages and combining them with the server-side templates. As a result of these models, CSS structures will further coordinate and enforce complex components. When utilizing CSS models, these components may also be used to format the pages dynamically.

1.12 Handling Flash Animation and Effects

Flash components may be explicitly placed and treated on a website using CSS Flash files. In CSS, there are built-in frameworks and style sheets that can be used to manage the case. The animations can be made directly in the frameworks, and the results can be modified. With the support of assets, the requisite flash files can be processed and applied to produce movies and animation on web pages.

1.13 End-User and Server-Side Representation

CSS files can communicate directly with the user's server-side answer and be used for interphase styling on the webserver. It makes it possible to create better online representations from the viewpoint of the end-user.

1.14 Editors with CSS

CSS stands for Cascading Style Sheets and is a common style sheet language in the IT world. It's a term that describes how websites or documents look. CSS is usually used in conjunction with JavaScript and HTML.

Web designers use a CSS editor to make improvements to a.css file quickly and effortlessly. The same technique may efficiently decipher the file, making it easier to find mistakes and typos.

CSS editors come in a variety of shapes and sizes. Some are paid business resources, and some are free and open-source. Using the CSS editor (open-source) may be advantageous in a variety of situations.

It may be anything from collaborating with architects and engineers on a full-fledged project or designing one's website.

Before we move into the arguments of why you can use an CSS editor (open-source), let's examine why CSS is a better tool for web pages than HTML.

Why is CSS used for appearance rather than HTML?

While HTML can be used to determine the appearance of web pages on its own, CSS allows the whole process much simpler and more effective.

Developers may represent different improvements around a website using a single.css file. Using HTML to do this necessitates making individual modifications to HTML files (web page), not a viable choice.

Alert: Open-Source is not the same as free.

People always mix up free software and freeware with open-source. Please be aware that the two are related but not identical. Open-source coding tools allow developers to import and edit the source code when accessing the software for free.

While free software tools are entirely free to use, they do not allow for installing and modifying their source code. Several CSS editors are available for download, but they are not open-source. Coffee-Cup Style-Sheet Maker and Simple-CSS are two examples.

1.15 The Benefits of Using an Open-Source CSS Editor

There are several compelling reasons to use an open-source best CSS editor for your project. The most critical are:

- Collaboration with coworkers is simple

Since there are no permits for multi-use, using an open-source CSS editor allows you to share freely with coworkers. Furthermore, unlike shareware or demo variants of tools, open-source tools do not have a cap on the number of participants or a time limit.

- Personalize according to the needs

Per project has its own set of goals and specifications. As a result, the one-size-fits-all approach would not seem to be appropriate in this situation. Thankfully, open-source CSS editors allow developers and teams to customize the code to meet their needs.

- Active Participation of the Community

Any topics necessitate a conversation with a seasoned professional. Most open-source software, CSS editors included, have a vibrant, growing group that is still willing to lend a hand to those in need. When faced with ventures that have specific criteria, it can be your best option.

1.16 CSS Editors

The Atom

Available for the following operating systems:

- Linux RedHat or Ubuntu

- macOS 10.9 or later

- Windows 7 or later

- GitHub Developer

February 2014 was the first time the book was published.

It's been dubbed "A hackable text editor for the twenty-first century." Atom is one of the most common open-source code editors on the market today. It includes many of the functionality that a developer would anticipate from a code editor, such as autocompletion, file system browsing and support for various programming languages.

The Atom's most notable feature is that it allows real-time teamwork even easier and more profitable. Atom's cross-platform capability is due to the Electron platform on which it is built.

Furthermore, Atom comes with a long list of packages that enhance the text editor's capabilities and functionality. The Atom group has developed and selected themes that can be included in the fancy text editor.

Brackets

Available for the following operating systems:

- Linux Mint or Ubuntu

- macOS 10.14 or later

- Windows 7 or later

- Adobe Systems (original) and Adobe (original) are the developers (present)

November 2014 was the first time the game was published.

Adobe's Brackets is another prominent CSS editor in the developer community. Brackets is a front-end development and web design platform with an emphasis on graphic tools and preprocessor assistance. Brackets have several advantages, one of which is their lightweight.

Brackets have a live preview option that enables you to see updates to the website when created. With support for plugins, the code editor also allows for a certain amount of modification.

Inline editors are a fascinating function of Brackets that eliminate the need to switch between file tabs by opening an inline window you consider the most relevant. Oh, and the code editor is available in more than 35 different languages.

Notepad++

It is compatible with Windows 7 and older.

Don Ho is the developer.

November 2003 was the first time the book was published.

Notepad++ is the second-most common code editor, according to the 2019 Stack Overflow Developer Survey. Notepad++ is the preferred code editor for developers worldwide who prefer an easy, lightweight, and extensible code editor for Windows. Notepad++, which is written in C++, has an incredible combination of speed and limited scale. The code editor accomplishes this by using the pure Win32 API and STL.

Many of the standard code editor tools, such as autocompletion, locate and substitute, and tabbed editing, are included in Notepad++. The code editor supports over 20 different programming languages, making it one of the most powerful code editors on the market.

Kamoda Edit:

It is compatible with

• Linux CentOS, Fedora, OpenSUSE, Red Hat Enterprise Linux, SUSE Linux Enterprise, or Ubuntu

• Windows XP or later

• macOS 10.9 or later

Active State was released in January 2007 as a developer's first release.

Komodo Edit is a stripped-down version of the famous Komodo IDE's code editor. The code editor is preferred for various programming languages, including JavaScript, Perl, PHP, Python, Ruby, SQL, and XML, in addition to CSS.

The code editor for dynamic programming languages, Komodo Edit 4.3, is developed on top of the Open Komodo project.

Plugins and macros allow for customization. The former is built on the Mozilla Add-ons platform.

Unfortunately, the code editor lacks a live preview option. It also doesn't allow for real-time communication. On the other hand, Komodo Edit has a strong Go to Something function that allows you to navigate to any part of the source code quickly.

Visual Studio Code

It is available for the following operating systems:

• Linux Debian, Fedora, RedHat, SUSE, or Ubuntu

• macOS

• Windows 7 or older

Microsoft Initial Release - April 2015 Developer

According to the 2019 Stack Overflow Developer Survey, Visual Studio Code is the most common code editor. As a result, it has many functionalities that a developer might like in a code editor. It involves syntax highlighting, code refactoring, and autocompletion.

Debugging is usually not available in code editors. It is not the case for Visual Studio Code, which comes with a built-in debugger. Extensions, colors, keyboard shortcuts, and settings will all be used to customize the code editor.

Furthermore, the intelligent code completion function of Visual Studio Code is not the same as the standard autocomplete feature. Based on a functional specification, imported modules, and variable forms, it completes the code. Another explanation why it's the most famous option.

Bluefish

It is available for the following operating systems:

• macOS

• OpenSolaris

• Windows XP or later

• Linux ALT Linux, Debian, Fedora, Gentoo Linux, Slackware, or Ubuntu

Bluefish Dev Team was the first to release the game in 1997.

Bluefish is a simple-to-use but strong CSS editor. It's a powerful text editor with a slew of features for programming and creating interactive websites. It is suggested for developers searching for a straightforward method that does just as it says on the tin.

The code editor supports Ada, C, C++, Go, Java, PHP, Python, XML, and many other languages in addition to CSS. While Bluefish is a stand-alone program, it can also be used in conjunction with the GNOME desktop environment.

The code editor has a wizards option, and the standard code editing features like autocomplete and syntax highlighting. It's a fantastic function for getting things done quickly. There's also a programming-code-aware inline spell checker and a Unicode character browser.

Scintilla

Available for:

• macOS 10.6 or later

• MorphOS

• GTK+

• Unix-like

• Windows NT or a later version of Windows

Neil Hodgson is the developer.

May 1999 was the first time the game was published.

This entry, unlike the others on this series, is not a code editor. On the other hand, Scintilla is a free and open-source library with a text editing component that focuses on advanced source code editing capabilities.

On the other hand, Scintilla's code editing prowess will effectively compete with a dedicated code editor, which is why it's on the list. The Scintilla editor component is used for the extremely common Notepad++ code editor.

Syntax highlighting in Scintilla is not exclusive to fixed-Height fonts. It may also include autocompletion and code folding capabilities applied to it. The code editing component includes a simple regular expression search implementation in addition to error indicators and syntax decoration.

1.17 CSS Benefits and Disadvantages

The below are the benefits and drawbacks:

The Benefits

The following are the benefits mentioned:

- Compatibility with Devices

- Improved website performance

- Easy to keep up with

- Improvements that are both consistent and random

- The ability to reposition yourself

- Improves the ability of search engines to index web pag es

Consequences

The below are the drawbacks:

- Problems with cross-browser compatibility

- Susceptible

- Problems caused by different layers

- A lack of safety

- Disintegration

Chapter-2: What is CSS, and How Does It Work?

CSS interacts with HTML components to add charm to the web pages. Elements are the actual HTML elements of a web page, such as a paragraph, which look like this in HTML:

`</P> This is the beginning of my paragraph! </P>`

If you needed this paragraph to appear pink and bold to people who were reading your website from a web browser, you could use CSS code like this:

`A={color: red; font-weight: bold; }`

The "selector" in this case is "A" (This is the beginning of my paragraph!), which is the part of CSS code that specifies which HTML feature the CSS styling would influence. The selector appears to the left of the first curly bracket in CSS. A declaration is a knowledge within curly brackets that includes properties and values added to the selector. Font scale, color, and margins are examples of properties, while values are the settings for certain properties. "Color" and "font-weight" are all properties in the illustration above, whereas "red" and "bold" are values. The whole bracketed list of

`A {color: Red; Font weight: bold}`

Above statement is declaration, and "A" (is the paragraph of HTML) is the selector once more. Adjust margin indentations, background colors, font sizes, and more using the same fundamental concepts as an example.

`B { background-color: blue;}`

It would leave the color of the page blue

`A{font-weight:20px; color: White;}`

It will produce a White-letter paragraph in a 20-point font.

2.1 CSS applications

However, you may be wondering how this CSS coding is extended to HTML text. CSS, like HTML, is written in plain text using a text editor or word processor on your device, and there are three key ways to incorporate it into your HTML websites.

Inline:

An inline style sheet only affects the tag on which it is placed. It simply ensures that minor information on the website can be modified without affecting the page's overall appearance or anything on it. It is advantageous because if it were on the external pages, you'd have to put extra tags to alter information. Since inline takes precedence over external, minor information may be modified. It also takes precedence over the internal.

Finally, inline styles are CSS fragments written directly into HTML code that is only accessible to one instance of coding. Consider the following scenario:

Take a look at this headline!

`<h1 style="font-size:10px; color: orange;">Consider the example!`
`</h1>`

It will have one particular headline show in orange, 10-point font on a single.html tab.

Internal

Only use the internal if you only choose to make a minor modification to a specific name. Inline affects the one tag found inside it, while internal style is applied to the HTML document's head. It ensures that you will display all of the necessary modifications through scrolling if you want to edit the page. External styling is included inside the marks. Because of the different style and tagging, this seems neater, plain, sleek, and ordered. CSS directives written directly into the header of a specific.html file are known as internal style sheets. It is particularly helpful if your platform has a single page with a distinct look. It is an example of an internal style sheet.

<head>

<style>

Body {background-color: Red;}

P {font-size:14px; color: blue;}

</style>

</head>

This page will have a red background and 14 font sizes with blue color.

```html
ne.html ☒
 1    <!DOCTYPE html>
 2    <html>
 3    <head>
 4      <title>Internal CSS Style</title>
 5      <style type="text/css">
 6        p {
 7          color:purple;
 8          margin-left:20px;
 9        }
10        div{
11          color:purple;
12          font-size:16px;
13          background-color:#FF6633;
14        }
15      </style>
16    </head>
17    <body>
18      <p>This is a first paragraph.</p>
19      <div>This is a second paragraph.</div>
20    </body>
21    </html>
22
```

The output of this code will be like

This is a first paragraph.

This is a second paragraph.

External

People use external stylesheets to format and reconstruct their web pages on a completely different text. As more than one stylesheet can be inserted within the book, you can essentially have two or more workplaces, resulting in a much cleaner workspace. Under this scenario, the stylesheet will be readily available, which is a big benefit. Still, any modifications made to the external sheet will impact any of the parent sheets connected.

External-style sheets (.css files) may be used to monitor the presentation of a whole web page with only one file (rather than embedded the instances of CSS code to the HTML element you want to adjust). aligned to use an external-style sheet, you must have the header segment in your.html files that connects to the external-style sheet, that looks like this:

```
<head>
<link        rel="        stylesheet"        type="text/Habib"
href=my.web.page.css">
</head>
```

It would connect the.html file to the external-style sheet (in this case, my.web.page.css),

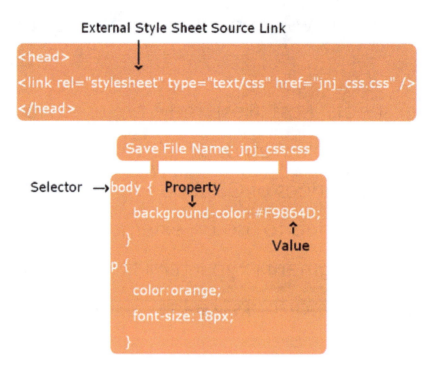

External Style Sheet Source Link

```
<head>
<link rel="stylesheet" type="text/css" href="jnj_css.css" />
</head>
```

Save File Name: jnj_css.css

Selector → body { Property
          background-color: #F9864D;
                              ↑
          }   Value
p {

    color:orange;

    font-size:18px;

    }

Begin by creating an HTML file with an embedded style board,
such as this one

```
ne.html ⊠
1     <!DOCTYPE HTML>
2   ⊟<html>
3   ⊟<head>
4     <meta charset="UTF-8">
5     <title>Embedded Style Sheet</title>
6   ⊟<style>
7       h1 {
8         color: #009;
9         font-size: 1em;
10        margin-bottom: .3em;
11        text-align: center;
12        text-decoration: underline;
13      }
14
15      table {
16        margin: .3em;
17        width: 290px;
18      }
19
20      th {
21        padding: .2em;
22      }
23
24      td {
25        background-color: #ffc;
26        border: 1px solid #900;
27        padding-left: .5em;
28        padding-right: .5em;
29      }
30
31      #trHeader {
32        color: #900;
33        text-decoration: underline;
34      }
35
36      . center Cell {
37        text-align: center;
38      }
39    </style>
40    </head>
```

```
41  <body>
42
43  <div>
44    <h1>All-time Home Run Record</h1>
45    <table>
46      <tr id="trHeader">
47        <th>Student</th>
48        <th>Home Marks</th>
49        <th>School</th>
50      </tr>
51      <tr>
52        <td>HABIB</td>
53        <td class="centerCell">762</td>
54        <td>Greenhood Public School</td>
55      </tr>
56      <tr>
57        <td>Asalam</td>
58        <td class="centerCell">755</td>
59        <td>Scope School</td>
60      </tr>
61      <tr>
62        <td>Akbar</td>
63        <td class="centerCell">714</td>
64        <td>Fasial Model School </td>
65      </tr>
66      <tr>
67        <td>Yasir </td>
68        <td class="centerCell">660</td>
69        <td>Royel Kids School </td>
70      </tr>
71    </table>
72  </div>
73  </body>
74  </html>
75
```

Please make a new file called Style_Sheet.css and store it in the same directory. (As long as the file has the.css filename, you can call it anything you want.)

```css
new.css
1   h1 {
2       text-align: center;
3       font-size: 1em;
4       color: #009;
5       margin-bottom: .3em;
6       text-decoration: underline;
7   }
8
9   table {
10      margin: .3em;
11      width: 290px;
12  }
13
14  th {
15      padding: .2em;
16  }
17
18  td {
19      padding-left: .5em;
20      padding-right: .5em;
21      border: 1px solid #900;
22      background-color: #ffc;
23  }
24
25  #trHeader {
26      text-decoration: underline;
27      color: #900;
28  }
29
30  .centerCell {
31      text-align: center;
32  }
33
```

Both CSS files can be moved from the HTML file to the StyleSheet.css file. The type tags cannot be copied.

Delete the HTML block(style).

In the HTML file, after the closing title tag add a link tag that points to Style_Sheet.css.

`<link href="Style_Sheet.css" rel="style_sheet">`

Characteristics include:

href	Shows to the location of the sheet (external style)
rel	Should be added to "style-sheet" for linking style-sheets
type	Should be added to "text/Habib" for linking to CSS

Browse this will produce the following output

HABIB¤	762¤	¤	Greenhood·Public·School¤
Asalam¤	755¤	¤	Scope·School¤
Akbar·¤	714¤	¤	Fasial·Model·School¤
Yasir¤	660¤	¤	Royel·Kids·School¤

External-style sheets are the most effective solution for applying CSS on a website (it's simpler to monitor and apply a site's style from a dedicated CSS file). However, internal style sheets and inline style can be utilized on a case-by-case basis where individual style adjustments are required.

Any rule specified in the external style-sheet file takes precedence, and rules defined in this file may only be followed where the above two rules are not valid.

CSS Selectors

The browser interprets a CSS rule and applies it to the relevant elements in our HTML code. There are three parts to a style rule:

- A selector is a tool that can be used to "find" (or select) HTML elements based on their entity name, id, class, attribute, and other criteria.

- A CSS property is a kind of CSS design. Tone, border, backdrop, font, window, text orientation, margins, line spacing, and so on are all possibilities.

- Properties are given value. The background-color property, for example, may be red or green.

2.2 Basic function and their syntax of CSS

Font Properties

Font-Family

The following statement is used to change the font family.

`P {font-family: "Habib Public School", Calibri, Sans-serif;}`

Font-Style

The following statement is used to Change text, normal, oblique, and italics.

`H2 {font-style: italics;}`

`H1 {font-style: oblique;}`

Font-Variant

The following statement is used to display font in normal or small-caps.

`SPAN {font-variant: small-caps;}`

Font-Weight

The following statement is used to specify the weight of the font.

`H1 {font-weight: 500;}`

Or

`P {font-weight: normal;}`

Font-Size

The following statement is used to modify the size of the displayed font.

`H1 {font-size: Small;} or P {font-size: 14pt;}`

`LI {font-size: 90%;}`

`STRONG {font-size: Smaller;}`

Font

The following statement is used to combine all properties of fonts.

`P {font:  bold 17pt/18pt Calibri, serif;}`

2.3. Color and Background Properties

Color

The following statement is used to Change the color of text.

`H1 {color: red;} or H2 {color: #001080;}`

Background-Color

The following statement is used to set the background color of an element.

`H3 {background-color: Green; }`

`BODY {background-color: #000180;}`

Background-Image

The following statement is used Sets the background image of an element.

`BODY {background-image: URL (/images/haib.png);}`

`P                              {background-image:                    URL (http://www.facebook.com/hg.png);}`

Background-Repeat

This property determines how a background picture is reproduced.

The object will be repeated horizontally with the repeat x.value, while the image will be repeated vertically with the repeat-y value.

`BODY {background: Red URL(babydoll.png);`

`background-repeat: repeat-x; }`

Background-Attachment

Determines whether a background picture would scroll with the text or remain locked on the canvas.

```
BODY {background: white URL(habib.gif);
background-attachment: fixed; }
```

Background

It is Used to combine all properties of background.

```
BODY                    {background:                    white
url(http://www.facebook.com/fow.gif); }
BLOCKQUOTE {background: #4fffd5; }
P {background: URL(../backgrounds/habib.png) #f0f9ff fixed; }
TABLE {background: red URL( scope.jpg) no-repeat bottom right;
}
```

2.4. Text Properties

Word-Spacing

It is used to defines an additional amount of space between words.

```
P EM {word-spacing: 0.5 em; }
P. note {word-spacing: -0.5em; }
```

Letter-Spacing

It is used to defines an additional amount of space between characters.

```
H1 {letter-spacing: 0.2em; }
```

```
P.note { letter-spacing: -0.2em; }
```

Text Decoration

Its aim is to enable text to be embellished using one of five prop erties: (underline, overline, line-through, blink, none.)

```
A: link, A: visited, A: active {text.1-decoration: none; }
```

Vertical-Align

```
IMG.middle { vertical-align: middle; }
```

```
IMG { vertical-align: 60%; }
```

```
. exponent {vertical-align: super; }
```

Text-Transform

Allows you to capitalize the first letter in each phrase (capitalize), capitalize any of a word's letters (uppercase), and include any tiny letters.

```
H1 {text-transform: lowercase;}
```

```
H2 {text-transform: uppercase;}
```

Text-Align

It allows is used to justify text left, center, right, and justify.

```
H1 {text-align: center;}
```

```
P .geonewz { text-align: justify; }
```

Text-Indent

It is use to specify the amount of indentation of text.

```
P { text-indent: 9em; }
```

Line-Height

It is Used to control the spacing between baselines of text.

```
P { line-height: 500%; }
```

2.5. Classification Properties

Type-of-List-Style If list-style image is none or image loading is disabled, this value specifies the kind of list-item marker to use.

```
LI. square {list-style-type: square;}
```

```
UL.plain { list-style.1-type: none; }
```

```
OL {list-style-type: upper-alpha;}
```

```
OL OL { list-style-type: decimal; }
```

```
OL OL OL { list-style-type: lower-roman; }
```

List-Style-Image

When picture loading is activated, this property specifies the image that will be used as the list-item marker, replacing the marker defined in the list-style-type property.

```
UL.chap { list-style-image: url(/LI-mark/chap-mark.gif); }
```

```
UL LI.x { list-style-image: url(x.png); }
```

List-Style-Position

Determines where the marker is placed in regard to the list item. If the value inside is used, the lines will wrap under the marker instead of being indented. outside is default.

```
UL { list-style-position: inside; }
```

Margin-Top

Sets an element's top margin by setting a duration or a percentage.

```
H1 { margin-top: 15pt; }
```

Margin-Right

Sets an element's appropriate right margin by setting a duration or a percentage.

```
H2 { margin-right: 50%; }
```

Margin-Bottom

specifies a period or a percentage for an element's bottom margin.

`HG { margin-bottom: 6 em; }`

Margin-Left

Sets an element's appropriate   left margin by setting a duration or a percentage.

`Post { margin-left: 40%; }`

2.6. Box Properties

Margin

Sets an element's margin by determining top, bottom, left, and right margins, both of which may be specified in either duration or percentage.

Set All margins 12em

`BODY {margin: 12em; }`

Set top & bottom 2em, left & right 4em

`P {margin: 2em 4em; }`

Set top-margin 2em, right 3em, bottom 2em, left 5em

`DIV {margin: 2em 3em 2em 5em; }`

Padding-Top

The distance between the content of the selector   and the top border is defined by this value.

`P {padding top: 50%; }`

Padding-Right

The distance between   the data of the selector the correct borders is specified by this value.

`P {padding-right: 60 px;}`

Padding-Bottom

The gap between the bottom border as well as the content of t he selector is defined by this value.

`P {padding-bottom: 10 em; }`

Padding-Left

The distance between   the data of the selector   the left borders is specified by this value.

`P {padding-left: 25 pt;}`

Padding

The padding-right,   padding-top, padding-left characteristics, padding-bottom, and are shortened as padding-top, padding-right, padding-bottom, and padding-left.

```
BQ {padding: 4em 5em 6em 5em; }
```

Border-Top-Height

The height of an object top border is specified by:

```
A {border-top: 25%; }
```

Border-Right-height

The Height of an object right border is specified by:

```
A{border-right: 25%;}
```

Border-Bottom-Height

The Height of an object's bottom border is specified by:

```
A {border-bottom: 25%;}
```

Border-Left-Height

The Height of an element's left border is specified by:

```
A {border-left: 25%; }
```

Border-Height

The Height of an element's boundary is set with this property (eit her all borders, or specifying top border, right border, bottom bo rder, left border).

```
A {border-Height: 25%;}
```

```
A {border-Height: 15px 15 px 15px 15 px;}
```

Border-Color

The color of an element's boundary is fixed by

`A {border-color: #00005;}`

Border-Style

Sets the border type, which may be zero, dotted, striped, flat, or double.

`A {border-style: dotted;}`

Border-Top

The top border of an entity is described by its distance, shape, and color.

`A {border-top: 15px, blue, double;}`

Border-Right

The distance, shape, and color of an object right border are all adjustable.

`A {border-right: 15px, blue, double;}`

Border-Bottom

The distance, shape, and colour of an element's bottom border are all customizable.

`A {border-bottom: 15px, bule, double;}`

Border-Left

The distance, shape, and colour of an element's left border are all customizable.

```
A {border-left: 15px, blue, double; }
```

Border

The distance, style, and color of an element's border are all adjustable.

```
A {border: 15px, Blue, double; }
```

Height

A Height may be defined as a length, a percentage, or auto for each block-level or substituted unit.

```
A {Height: 15px;}
```

```
H2 {Height: 35%;}
```

```
.fo {Height: auto;}
```

Height

A height can be specified for each block

level or substituted unit, either as a duration or as auto.

```
A {height: 15px; }
```

```
H2 {height: 35%; }
```

```
.fo {height: auto; }
```

Float

Allows you to wrap text around an item (left, right, none).

```
A { float: left; }
```

```
H2 { float: right; }
```

```
.fo { float: none; }
```

Clear

Whether or not an element requires floating elements to be pla ced on its sides (left, right, none).

```
A {clear: left;}
```

```
H2 {clear: right;}
```

```
.fo {clear: none;}
```

Chapter-3: Rules

CSS selectors are used to "dig" (or choose) the HTML elements to style.

CSS selectors are divided into five categories:

- Basic selectors (select elements based on name, id, class)

- Selectors for combinators (select elements based on a specific relationship between them)

- Selectors for pseudo-classes (select elements based on a certain state)

- Selectors for pseudo-elements (select and style a part of an element)

- Selectors for attributes (select elements based on an attribute or attribute value)

The most basic CSS selectors will be explained in the following example.

```
<!DOCTYPE html>
<html>
<head>
<style>
p {
  color: red;
  text-align: center;
}
</style>
</head>
<body>

<p>Hi Good Morning!</p>
<p>I am writing this paragraph to explain seclector. In this p is a
Selectors.</p>

</body>
</html>
```

The results

Hi Good Morning!

I am writing this paragraph to explain seclector. In this p is a Selectors.

3.1. Selectors for Classes

A simple selector may have several groups, enabling various styles to be applied to the same feature. e.g., based on the language, an author may choose to view code in a different color:

```
code.html {color: #092980}
```

```
code.css {color: #4c0081}
```

For use with HTML's CODE feature, the above example of code has provided two groups, CSS and HTML. It's also possible to declare a class without a related element:

`. note {font-size: small}`

In this situation, the **note** class can be used with any element.

It's a smart idea to name groups based on their functionality rather than their looks. The notice class in the preceding illustration may have been slim, but that name would be useless if the author changed the class's type to no longer have a tiny font size. Both HTML items with the class="center" will be red and center-aligned in this example:

```
<!DOCTYPE html>
<html>
<head>
<style>
.center {
  text-align: center;
  color: red;
}
</style>
</head>
<body>

<h1 class="center">Red and center-aligned heading</h1>
<p class="center">Red and center-aligned paragraph.</p>

</body>
</html>
```

3.2. Selectors for IDs

On an element-by-element basis, ID selectors are allocated individually. Due to its inherent limitations, this selector style should be used only when required. The indicator "#" is used to precede a name when creating an ID selector. An ID selector, for example, maybe set up as follows:

```html
<!DOCTYPE html>
<html>
<head>
<style>
#para1 {
  text-align: center;
  color: red;
}
</style>
</head>
<body>

<p id="para1">Hi Good Morning!</p>
<p>This paragraph is not affected by the style.</p>

</body>
</html>
```

3.3. Contextual Selectors

Contextual Selectors are a form of contextual selectors used in Strings with two or more basic selectors divided by white space make up contextual selectors. These selectors may be given normal properties, and they will take priority over basic selectors due to the rules of cascading order. The contextual selector, for example, in

`P EM {background: yellow}` is a P EM

This rule states that stressed text inside a paragraph should be set against a yellow background; nevertheless, emphasized text in a heading is unchanged.

3.4. Grouping

Grouping of selectors and declarations is required in style sheets to reduce the number of repetitive phrases. E.g., a grouping may be used to offer all of the headings in a document the same declaration:

```
H1, H2, H3, H4, H5, H6 {
  color: red;
  font-family: sans-serif}
```

3.5. Inheritance

Unless otherwise specified, all selectors that are nested inside selectors will inherit the property values assigned to the outer selector. A color specified for the BODY, for example, would be added to the text.

There are a few instances where the selector is not inherited by the outer selector values of the surrounding selector, although they should be obvious. The margin-top attribute, for example, is not inherited; a column does not have the same top margin as the paper body.

3.6. Remarks

Inside style sheets, comments are indicated using the same conventions as in C programming. A typical CSS statement will look like this:

```
/* COMMENTS Should not be nested */
```

3.7. CSS Rules Overriding

We've gone through four different approaches to applying style sheet rules to our HTML code. To circumvent every Style Sheet Regulation, use the following rule:

<style>...</style>

The preference is given to every inline style mat. As a result, any rule specified in tags or rules defined in any external style-sheet file would be overridden.

Any rule specified in tags would take precedence over any rules defined in an external style-sheet.

Any rule specified in the external style-sheet file takes precedence, and rules defined in this file may only be followed where the above two rules are not valid.

3.8. CSS Selectors

The browser interprets a CSS rule and applies it to the relevant elements in our HTML code. There are three sections of a style rule:

- A selector is a tool that can be used to "find" (or select) HTML elements based on their entity name, id, class, attribute, and other criteria.

- A CSS property is a kind of CSS design. Tone, border, backdrop, font, window, text orientation, margins, line spacing, and so on are all possibilities.

- Properties are given value. The background-color property, for example, maybe either red or green.

3.9. Syntax of CSS Rules

A CSS law has two parts: a selector and a statement of property and value:

Selector {property: value;}

The selector identifies the HTML feature that needs to be styled.

One or two statements are divided by semicolons in the declaration block (in curly braces).

A colon separates the name of the CSS property and its meaning in each declaration.

A CSS rule may be written once and then reused in several HTML elements and papers. We don't need to write HTML inline tag attributes any time we use CSS because they apply to the styled variable. We write a single CSS rule and extend it to all instances of the tag variable. As a result, fewer lines of code equal faster websites.

When we use external or embedded style rules, making changes and maintaining our HTML document is a breeze. All items in our HTML documents would be automatically changed if we modify the style rule. We may use Media Queries in CSS to reach a variety of display screen sizes. We will use media queries to configure our HTML document for several types of devices. We may display various versions of our web pages using the same HTML code.

3.10. Overriding CSS Rules

We've gone over three different approaches to applying style sheet rules to our HTML code. To circumvent every Style Sheet Regulation, use the following rule:

The preference should be given to every inline style mat. As a result, any rule specified in the <style>.... </style> tags, as well as rules defined in any external style-sheet format, would be overridden.

Any rule specified in <style>.../style> tags take precedence over any rules defined in an external style-sheet format.

3.11. Pseudo-elements and Pseudo-classes

Pseudo-classes and pseudo-elements are unique "classes" and "elements" that CSS-supporting browsers know immediately. Pseudo-classes differentiate between various element forms (e.g., visited links and active links represent two types of anchors). Sub-parts of components, such as the first letter of a text, are referred to as pseudo-elements.

The type of rules with pseudo-classes or pseudo-elements is

`selector:pseudo-class { property: value }`

or

`selector:pseudo-element { property: value }`

The CLASS attribute in HTML cannot be used to specify pseudo-classes or pseudo-elements. Pseudo-classes and pseudo-elements may be used together in the following way:

`selector.class:pseudo-class { property: value }`

or

```
selector. class: pseudo-element { property: value }
```

3.12. Pseudo-classes as anchors

The A entity may be given pseudo-classes to view links, visited links, and active links differently. The pseudo-classes relation visited, and activities can all be assigned to the anchor element. A visited connection could be assigned a different color and different font size and design.

A fun result will be to show a currently selected (or "active") connection in slightly larger font size and a different color. The visited connection then appears in smaller font size and a different color when the page is re-selected. The below is an example of a style sheet:

```
X: link {color: Orange}
```

```
X: active {color: red; font-size: 90%}
```

```
X: visited {color: blue; font-size: 90%}
```

3.13. Pseudo-element in the First Line

The first line of text in newspaper papers, such as that in the Wall Street Journal, is often written in bold lettering and all caps. This functionality was used as a pseudo-element in CSS1. Any block-level entity will use a first-line pseudo-element (such as P, H1, etc.). A first-line pseudo-element might look like this:

```
Z: first-line {
  font-variant: small-caps;
  font-weight: bold}
```

3.14. Pseudo-element (first letter)

Drop caps and other effects are created using the first-letter pseudo-element. The meaning allocated to the first letter of text inside an assigned selector would be made. Any block-level entity will use a first-letter pseudo-element. Get the next case:

```
P: first-letter {font-size: 300%; float: left}
```

The will result in a drop cap three times the size of the standard font.

3.15. Cascading Order

When using several style sheets, the style sheets can compete for control of a certain selector. There must be guidelines in place that determine which style sheet's law would take precedence in these cases. The following characteristics can determine the result of inconsistent style sheets.

Important

The! important keyword may be used to mark a rule as essential. A style that has been marked as significant will triumph over styles that are otherwise similar in weight. Similarly, since both the author and the reader will specify essential laws, the author's law would precede the readers in important situations. Here's an example of how to use the! essential statement:

```
BODY {background: URL(Gaf.gif) white;
 background-repeat: repeat-x! important}
```

3.16.Origin of Rules

Both writers and readers, as previously said, have the right to specify style sheets. Where the author's rules and the reader's rules differ, the author's rules may take precedence over the reader's rules, which are otherwise identical in weight. The style sheets of both the author and the viewer circumvent the browser's built-in style sheets.

Authors can avoid utilizing! Essential rules so they can circumvent some! important rules set by the user. Due to vision issues, a user can need huge font sizes or specific colors, and such a user will certainly declare certain design laws to be! Relevant, since certain types are required for the user to read a page. Since some! essential laws can circumvent normal rules, writers can almost only use normal rules to guarantee that people with special style requirements will read the page.

Calculating Specificity Using Selector Rules

Conflicting design sheets may also be overridden depending on their degree of detail, with a more detailed template often winning out over a less specific one. Calculating the specificity of a selector is simply a counting game.

- Count how many ID attributes there are in the selector.

- Count how many CLASS attributes there are in the selector.

- Count how many HTML tag names there are in the selector.

Finally, to get a three-digit figure, compose the three digits in exact sequence with no spaces or commas. (Note that to get three digits, you can need to translate the numbers to a larger base.) Specificity can be conveniently determined from the final list of numbers referring to selectors, with higher numbers winning out over lower numbers. A collection of selectors is given below, ordered by specificity:

```
#id1      {x.x.x.} /* x=2 y=0 z=3 --> specificity = 203 */
```

```
UL UL LI.red {x.x.x} /* x=3 y=0 z=3 --> specificity = 303 */
```

```
LI.red      {x.x.x.} /* x=2 y=2 z=1 --> specificity = 211 */
```

```
LI          {x.x.x.} /* x=2 y=3 z=1 --> specificity = 231 */
```

3.17. Specification Order

The last rule mentioned wins when two laws have the same weight.

Chapter-4: Beginner's Guide to Best Practices

CSS is a language that almost any developer has used at some stage. Though we can take it for granted, it is a versatile language with several complexities that can support (or hurt) our projects. Here are 30 of the strongest CSS methods to help you write better CSS and prevent expensive errors.

4.1. Make it easy to read

The readability of your CSS is crucial, even though most people don't realize why. Since you'll identify elements faster if your CSS is well-read, it would be far simpler to manage in the future. Furthermore, you never know who would need to look at the code in the future.

4.2. Maintain Consistency

Making sure the CSS is compatible goes hand and hand with having your code readable. You can start creating your own CSS "sub-language" that helps you to call items easily. We build those groups in virtually every style, and We call them by the same name every time. We use. caption-right correct to float pictures with a caption to the right, for example. Consider if you'll include underscores or dashes in your IDs and class titles, as well as when and how you'll use them. You'll get even more proficient as you start making your CSS specifications.

4.3. Start with a Framework

Use a System Some architecture purists balk at the idea of utilizing a CSS framework for each design. Still, we agree that why reinvent the wheel while everyone else has taken the time to maintain a method that speeds up production? We understand that systems cannot be included in every situation. However, they can be useful in most cases.

Many designers have developed their systems over time, which is indeed a smart concept. It aids in maintaining project continuity.

Around the same time, we would like to point out that frameworks can only be used if you have a solid understanding of CSS. You'll almost definitely have to build a certain feature of a layout on your own at some stage, and your thorough knowledge of CSS will assist you in doing so.

4.4. Perform a Reset

Most CSS systems have a reset, so if you're not going to use it, at the very least, think about it. Browser anomalies such as heights, font styles, borders, and headings are effectively eliminated after resetting your browser. The reset ensures that your interface is compatible with all browsers.

The Meyer Web is a tried-and-true reset. Get it back to normal. Another often used reset is CSS.

4.5. Use a top-down structure to organize the stylesheet.

It's a good idea to organize your stylesheet so that you can locate pieces of your code easily. A top-down approach that addresses types as they emerge in the source code is suggested. As an example, a stylesheet could be organized as follows:

- Classes (body, a, p, h1, etc.)

- #header

- #nav-menu

- #main-content

4.5. Mix and Match Elements

The properties of elements in a stylesheet are also shared. Why not merge the previous coding instead of rebuilding it? Your h1, h2, and h3 components, for example, might all have the same font and color:

```
h1, h2, h3 {font-family: Courier New, color: #333}
```

If we chose, we might apply special characteristics to each of these header types (i.e., h1 {size: 2.1em}) later in the stylesheet

4.6. First, make the HTML.

Often programmers write CSS at the same time as they write HTML. While it will seem unnecessary to build both simultaneously, you can save even more time if you construct the HTML mockup first. This approach is used when you know all of your site's architecture elements but doesn't know what CSS you'll need for your template. Making the HTML layout first helps you see the whole page and learn of the CSS in a more holistic, top-down way.

4.7. Use a variety of classes

Adding several groups to an element may be useful at times. Let's presume you want to float a div "box" to the right, and you already have a .right in your CSS that floats all to the right. Introduce an additional class to the declaration, as follows:

```
<div class="box right"></div>
```

Any declaration may include as many groups as you like (space separated).

It is one of the instances where you could consider individual circumstances. While it is beneficial to use class names that indicate how they impact the style, you can stop utilizing class names that force you to move between HTML and CSS all of the time.

When using ids and class names like "left" and "back," be cautious. I'll use them, but just for stuff like blog post illustrations. Why is that? Let's say you decide down the line that you'd like to see the box float to the left. In this situation, you'd need to go back to the HTML to update the class name to change the page's appearance. It is a grammatical error. Keep in mind that HTML is for markup and content. CSS is used to make it look nice.

4.8. Make Use of the Correct Doctype

The doctype declaration has a significant impact on whether or not the markup and CSS are correct. In reality, based on the doctype you announce, the whole look and feel of your site will alter dramatically.

A-List Apart has further information about which <!DOCTYPE html> to use. When making HTML5-based websites, you can easily start using them.

4.9. Make use of shorthand

When writing CSS, you can significantly reduce the size of your code by using shorthand. You may mix types in one line with items like padding, border, font, and others. A div, for example, may have the following styles:

```css
#crayon {
    margin-left:    12px;
    margin-right:   12px;
    margin-top: 12px;
}
```

You might put all types together in one section, like this:

```css
#crayon {
    margin: 5px 5 px 5px 5 px; // top, right, bottom, and left values, respectively.
}
```

4.10. Add a comment to your CSS

It's a good idea to comment on the code in bits, much like every other script. Simply type /* behind the comment and */ to close it, as seen below:

/* This is the method of adding CSS comment: */

4.11. Recognize the distinction between block and inline elements

Block elements are elements that, once declared, clear each line and cover the entire Height of the usable room. Inline components only take up as much room as they require, and they don't require the creation of a new line until they've been used.

The following are some examples of inline elements:

`em, img, br, span, a, img, br, input, abbr, acronym, strong`

And there are many block of the object:

`table ,div ,blockquote,,`
`h1,h2,h3,h4,h5,h6, p, ul, li, form, pre`

4.12. Organize Your Assets by Alphabet

Though this is a more amusing tip, it can be useful for fast scanning.

```
#habibz-candy {
color: #fff;
float: left;
```

```
font-weight:
height: 20px;
margin: 10;
padding: 10;
Height: 150px;
}
```

It is debatable because you have to give up pace in exchange for marginally better readability. However, if you believe it would benefit you, you can give it a shot.

4.13. Use CSS Compressors

CSS compressors reduce the size of CSS files by eliminating line breaks, white spaces, and merging components. This combination will significantly minimize file size, resulting in faster tab loading. CSS Minifier and HTML Compressor are two great online CSS compression methods.

It's worth noting that although reducing the size of your CSS will improve consistency, it also reduces readability.

4.14. Make Generic Classes Work for You

We'll see that you're using the same styles over and over again. You may build generic classes and apply them to IDs or other CSS classes (using tip #8) instead of applying the specific style to each ID.

e.g., In the designs, the CSS properties are frequently used float right and float: left, So you add the. Left and .right classes to my stylesheet and reference it in the components.

```
. left {float: left}
```

```
. right {float: right}
```

|

```
<div id="cool box" class="left">...</div>
```

You won't have to keep adding float: left to all the elements that need to be floating this way.

4.15. Use to Center Layouts

Many CSS newbies are perplexed as to why you can't just use float: center on block-level items to achieve the focused impact. If only it were that easy! You'll have to use this approach to focus a div, paragraphs, or other elements in your style, unfortunately:

```
margin: 0 auto; // top, bottom - and left, right values, respectively.
```

By specifying that an element's left and right margins must be equal, browsers are forced to center the element inside its containing element.

4.16. Don't Just Wrap a div Around It

It's tempting to wrap an entity in a div with an ID or class and build a style for it when you're first starting.

```
<div class="header-text"><h1>Header Text</h1></div>
```

It can seem simpler to build specific element types, as in the illustration above, but this would clog up the stylesheet. It would have been perfect:

```
<h1>Header Text</h1>
```

Then, instead of using a parent div, you can apply a style to the h1.

4.17. Use the Developer Tools in Your Browser

Modern web browsers have several essential resources that every web developer should have. All of the main browsers, including Chrome, Firefox, Safari, and Edge, also have these development resources. You may visually examine, alter, and edit CSS in real-time using the Chrome and Firefox developer software, including monitoring JavaScript, testing HTML, and displaying errors.

4.18. Use Less Hacking

If at all practicable, avoid utilizing browser-specific hacks. There's a lot of demand to make sure that templates appear the same in all browsers, but utilizing hacks makes it difficult to preserve your designs in the future. Furthermore, utilizing a reset file will remove virtually all rendering inconsistencies across browsers.

4.19. Don't overuse absolute positioning.

Absolute positioning is a useful feature in CSS that enables you to specify the pixel where an element should be placed on a screen. However, since absolute positioning ignores other items on the web, templates may get very tangled if there are several completely placed elements strewn around.

4.20. Use Text-transform

text-transform is a CSS property that helps you to "standardize" the way text is formatted. For instance, let's assume you want to make some headers with just lowercase letters. Include the text-transform property in the header type as follows:

```
                                    text-transform:

            1                       lowercase;
```

By design, all of the letters in the header would be lowercase. With the text-transform property, you may change the case of the text (the 1st letter capitalized, all lowercase Or all letters capitalized,).

4.21. Don't Hide the H1 Tag with Negative Margins

People frequently use an icon for their header text and then float the h1 off the page with a display: none or a negative margin. Matt Catts, the head of Google's Webspam team at the time, has publicly stated that this is a poor idea because Google can mistake it for spam.

Avoid using CSS to hide the logo's text, as Catts specifically states. Simply utilizing the alt attribute. While some argue that CSS can also mask an h1 tag if the h1 is the same as the logo document.

4.22. Check the CSS and XHTML for errors.

Validating your CSS and XHTML gives you more than a feeling of accomplishment: it also allows you to identify errors in your code easily. If anything doesn't look correct when working on a template, consider running the markup and CSS validator to see what errors come up. Usually, you'll discover that you failed to close a div or that a semi-colon in a CSS property was missing.

4.23. Pixels vs. Rems and Ems

When determining font sizes, whether to use pixels (px) or ems and rems has often been a point of contention. Ems are more scalable for varying browser sizes and mobile devices than pixels, which are a more rigid way to describe font sizes. With the rise of many modes of web surfing (laptop, smartphone, etc.), ems and rems are gradually becoming the standard for font size dimensions since they have the most functionality.

4.24. Don't Take the List For Granted

Lists are a perfect way to view data in a standardized, easy-to-modify format. You don't have to use the array as a text attribute anymore, thanks to the view property. Lists are also useful for making navigation menus and other similar items.

Since they don't understand how to use lists properly, often beginners use div to create each variable in the list. It's well worth the time and effort to brush up on list components to further organize data in the future.

4.25. Don't Use Extra Selectors

It's quick to apply extra selectors to our CSS without realizing it, cluttering the stylesheet. Lists are a typical example of incorporating extra selectors.

```
body #container. Some_class ul li {....}
```

In this case, just using the. Some_class li would have sufficed.

```
Some_class li {...}
```

Adding extra selectors won't cause Armageddon, but they will prevent your CSS from being as quick and clean as possible.

4.26. Make All Elements Have Margins and Padding

Modern browsers render elements in a reasonably consistent manner, while legacy browsers render elements in a variety of ways. E.g., some things are rendered differently in Internet Explorer than in Firefox or Chrome, and various versions of Internet Explorer render differently.

Padding and borders are made differently in older browser models, one of the most noticeable variations. To be secure, if you're not still using a reset, you can specify the margin and padding for all items on the list. You can do this easily by doing a global reset, as seen below:

```
* {margin:0; padding:0;}
```

Until another style in the stylesheet specifies otherwise, all components now have padding and a margin of 0.

4.27. Make Use of Many Stylesheets

It's also simpler to render tiny, multiple stylesheets instead of one big stylesheet, depending on the sophistication of the concept and the scale of the platform. Multiple stylesheets encourage you to leave out CSS on pages that don't need it, in addition to making it easy for the designer to handle.

For instance, you could create a polling programmer with a distinct collection of styles. You might build a survey instead of using the poll styles in the main stylesheet. Just apply the CSS and stylesheet to the pages that show the poll.

However, keep in mind the total amount of HTTP requests being generated. Often artists tend to work with different stylesheets before combining them into a single document. The amount of HTTP requests is reduced to one. Additionally, the user's machine can archive the whole file.

4.28. When debugging, look for closed elements first.

If the template seems to be a little wonky, you've likely forgotten to have a closing. The XHTML validator will help you detect all kinds of errors like this.

4.29. Instead of using floats, try using Flexbox and Grid Layout.

In the past, using floats to construct some layout was very popular and appropriate. Floats, unfortunately, come with a slew of issues. Instead, it would be best if you started using the flexbox and grid layout modules, which are much more efficient. Flexbox can aid in creating one-dimensional layouts, while grid will aid in creating two-dimensional layouts.

Chapter-5: Starting with HTML And CSS

This chapter should guide you through learning CSS if you have never published before a CSS style sheet . It doesn't go into great detail about CSS.

It simply illustrates how to generate an HTML file and a CSS file and how to combine the two. After that, you can read any of a variety of codes to enhance the HTML and CSS files with additional functionality.

Alternatively, it would be best to use a dedicated HTML or CSS editor to create more sophisticated websites.

5.1. Let's get started on the HTML.

We're going to use the most basic resources for this part. For instance, Notepad (under Windows) will suffice. If you've mastered the fundamentals, you may want to move on to more sophisticated tools or even commercial software like Style Master, Dreamweaver, or Go Live. However, it's best not to get confused by so many advanced features while creating the first CSS style sheet. Using a word processor like Microsoft Word or OpenOffice instead. They usually create files that are inaccessible to a web browser. We want plain, quick text files for CSS & HTML.

Step 1: Open your editor (TextEdit, Notepad etc. whatever you prefer) and type the following into an empty window:

```html
new 1.html
1    <!DOCTYPE>
2    <html>
3    <head>
4      <title>My first styled page</title>
5    </head>
6
7    <body>
8
9    <!-- Site navigation menu -->
10   <ul class="navbar">
11     <li><a href="index.html">Home page</a>
12     <li><a href="musings.html">Musings</a>
13     <li><a href="town.html">My town</a>
14     <li><a href="links.html">Links</a>
15   </ul>
16
17   <!-- Main content -->
18   <h1>My first styled page</h1>
19
20   <p>Welcome to my styled page!
21
22   <p>It lacks images, but at least it has style.
23   And it has links, even if they don't go
24   anywhere & hell ip;
25
26   <p>There should be more here, but I don't know
27   what yet.
28
29   <!-- Sign and date the page, it's only polite! -->
30   <address>Made 21 April 2021<br>
31     by myself.</address>
32
33   </body>
34   </html>
```

Let's pretend this is a single page from a larger website containing many related sites. This page has a menu that connects to other pages on the hypothetical platform, some special material, and a signature typical of existing Web pages.

Now, from the File menu, click "Save As...", move to a directory/folder where you wish to save the file (the Desktop would suffice), and save the file as "New 1.html." We'll need the editor again, so don't shut it just yet. (If you're using TextEdit on a Mac OS X version before 10.4, you'll see an option.) In the Save as dialogue, leave the.txt extension off. Since the term "mypage.html" already has an extension, use that choice. The.html extension will be immediately detected in newer versions of TextEdit.) Then, in a tab, open the link. By following these steps, you will do so: Using the file manager (Windows Explorer, Finder, or Konqueror), locate the "mypage.html" file and double-click it. Your default Web browser should launch it. (If it doesn't launch automatically, open your tab and move the file there.) As you can see, the website seems to be quite dull...

5.2. Adding some colors

You'll likely see black text against a white screen, although that all depends on how your browser is set up. So, adding any colors to the page is a simple way to make it look cool. (Keep the tab open; we'll get back to it later.) We'll begin with an HTML file that includes a style sheet. We'll place the HTML and CSS in different files later. Separate files are beneficial since they enable you to reuse the same style sheet through several HTML files: you have to write the style sheet once. However, we will hold everything in one file for this move. In the file, we need to add a <style> feature. That factor will contain the style sheet. Return to the editor window and apply the following five lines to the HTML file's head section. In the package, you'll find the lines to add.

```
new 1.html
1    <!DOCTYPE>
2    <html>
3    <head>
4       <title>My first styled page</title>
5       <style type="text/css">
6       body {
7          color: purple;
8          background-color: #d8da3d }
9       </style>
10   </head>
11
12   <body>
13
```

According to the first paragraph, this is a style board written in CSS ("text-css"). We add style to the "body" part, according to the second line. The third line changes the text color to purple, and the next line changes the background color to a greenish-yellow. The document's background would be the same as the background of the body part. We haven't provided some of the other elements (p, li, address...) a context to have none by design (or: will be transparent). Unless expressly overridden, the 'color' property sets the color of the text for the body variable, but all other entities within the body inherit the color. (Other colors will be added later.)

Return to the browser window and save the file (using "Save" from the File menu). The view can shift from the "boring" page to a colored (but still very boring) page if you push the "Reload" icon. The text should now be purple against a greenish-yellow backdrop, except for the list of links at the end.

5.3. Adding fonts

Another simple way to do this is to differentiate the fonts used by the various elements of the page. So, except for the h1 heading, which will be placed in "Helvetica," let's set the text in "Georgia."Since you never know what fonts your readers have installed on their computers on the Internet, we include some alternatives: if Georgia isn't accessible, Times New Roman or Times are good, and if all else fails, the browser can use some other serif font. If Helvetica isn't accessible, Geneva, Arial, and Sun Sans Regular are all quite close in shape. If neither of these fit, the browser should use either serif-free font. Add the following lines to the text editor:

```
new 1.html ✖
 1    <!DOCTYPE>
 2    <html>
 3    <head>
 4        <title>My first styled page</title>
 5        <style type="text/css">
 6        body {
 7          font-family: Georgia, "Times New Roman",
 8                Times, serif;
 9          color: purple;
10          background-color: #d8da3d }
11        h1 {
12          font-family: Helvetica, Geneva, Arial,
13                SunSans-Regular, sans-serif }
14        </style>
15    </head>
16
17    <body>
18
```

If you save the file again and then hit the "Reload" button in you r window, the heading and the rest of the text should now be in separate fonts.

5.4. Adding a navigation bar

The top of the HTML page has a chart that will double as a navigation menu. Many Web pages have a menu at the top or to the side of the screen, and this page can do the same. We'll position it on the left side because it'll be more interesting there than on the right...

The menu has already been used on the HTML page. It's the top-level ul> list. Since our "Web site" so far consists of just one tab, the links in it don't function, but that doesn't matter right now. Of necessity, there should be no damaged tiles on a real website.

To make space for it, we'll switch the list to the left and most of the text a little to the west. We use the CSS properties 'padding-left (to transfer the body text) and 'position,' 'left,' and 'top' for this (to move the menu).

There are other options as well. Look for the words "column" or "style" on the tab. Add the following lines to the HTML file in the editor window:

```
new 1.html
1    <!DOCTYPE">
2    <html>
3    <head>
4        <title>My first styled page</title>
5        <style type="text/css">
6        body {
7          padding-left: 11em;
8          font-family: Georgia, "Times New Roman",
9                Times, serif;
10         color: purple;
11         background-color: #d8da3d }
12       ul.navbar {
13         position: absolute;
14         top: 2em;
15         left: 1em;
16         width: 9em }
17       h1 {
18         font-family: Helvetica, Geneva, Arial,
19               SunSans-Regular, sans-serif }
20     </style>
21   </head>
22
23   <body>
```

You can now see several connections to the left of the main text if you save the file again and reopen it in the window. That already seems to be a lot more fascinating.

5.5. Styling the links

The navigation menu also seems to be a collection rather than a menu. Let's dress it up a little. The list bullet will be removed, and the objects will be moved to the left, where the bullet was. We'll also add a white background and a black square to each piece. We still haven't said what the relation colors should be, so let's include that: Purple for sites that the user has previously seen and blue for links that the user hasn't seen yet.

```
1    <!DOCTYPE>
2   <html>
3   <head>
4       <title>My first styled page</title>
5       <style type="text/css">
6       body {
7         padding-left: 11em;
8         font-family: Georgia, "Times New Roman",
9               Times, serif;
10        color: purple;
11        background-color: #d8da3d }
12      ul.navbar {
13        list-style-type: none;
14        padding: 0;
15        margin: 0;
16        position: absolute;
17        top: 2em;
18        left: 1em;
19        width: 9em }
20      h1 {
21        font-family: Helvetica, Geneva, Arial,
22              SunSans-Regular, sans-serif }
23      ul.navbar li {
24        background: white;
25        margin: 0.5em 0;
26        padding: 0.3em;
27        border-right: 1em solid black }
28      ul.navbar a {
29        text-decoration: none }
30      a:link {
31        color: blue }
32      a:visited {
33        color: purple }
34      </style>
35  </head>
36
37  <body>
```

5.6. Adding a horizontal line

A horizontal rule separates the text from the signature at the bottom of the style sheet, and is the last change to the style sheet. To add a dotted line above the <address> part, we'll use 'border-top':

```
address {
margin-top: 1em;
padding-top: 1em;
border-top: thin dotted}
```

Our look is now final. Next, we'll look at how we can save the style sheet as a separate file such that it can be shared across several other pages.

We already have an HTML file with a style sheet embedded in it. However, as our site expands, we would most likely require more sites to have the same theme. There is a simpler way than copying the style sheet into every page: we can place the style sheet in a separate file and link it to all sites. We'll need to build another empty text file to make a style sheet file. To build an empty window, choose "New" from the File menu in the editor. (If you're using TextEdit, remember to use the Format menu to return it to plain text.)

5.6. Putting the style sheet in a separate file

Then, from the HTML file, copy and paste everything within the st yle> element into the new browser. Don't only duplicate the <sty

le> and </style> tags. They're part of HTML, not CSS. You can no w have the whole style sheet in the latest editor window:

```
body {
  padding-left: 11em;
  font-family: Times New Roman, "Georgia"
    Times New Roman, serif;
  color: Red;
  background-color: #d9da3d }
ul.nav.bar {
  list. style-type-1: none;
  padding: 0;
  margin: 0;
  position-1: absolute;
  top: 2em;
  left: 1em;
  Height: 12em }
h1 {
  font-family: Georgia,Time, Arial,
    SunSans-bold, sans-serif }
```

```css
ul.nav-bar li {
   background: white;
   margin: 0.1m 0;
   padding: 0.5em;
   border-right: 2em solid white }
ul.nav-bar a {
   text1-decoration: none}
a:link {
   color: Red}
a:visit {
   color: Red }
address {
   margin-top: 2em;
   padding-top: 3em;
   border-top: thick dotted}
```

Choose "Save As" from the menu, then save the design sheet as "mycode.css" in the same folder as the mywebpage.html file. return to the browser containing the HTML code . Remove all up to and including the </style> tag from the <style> tag and substitute it with a <link> feature, as follows:

```
<link rel="style_sheet" href="my_style.css">
```

It Instructs the browser to search for the style sheet in the file "mystyle.css," When no directory is specified, the browser will look in the same directory as the HTML file. You can notice no difference if you save the HTML file and reopen it in the browser: the website is always designed the same way, but the style now comes from an external file.

The next move is to upload both the mypage.html and mystyle.css files to your website. (Well, you may want to tinker with the first...)

However, how you do that is determined by your Internet service provider.

Chapter-6: Practical Examples

To start the form is one of the most straightforward HTML projects. In this project, we will create a simple survey form and then submit the data captured. You can open any text editor to write your code, and save the file .html extension. E.g. survey1.html

Simple form creation, input tags, checkboxes, radio buttons and other topics will be covered.

The project's source code is available here, along with the requisite tag descriptions.

You should try out different components one at a time and see if they function.

```html
1   <!DOCTYPE HTML>
2   <!-- This is how HTML comments look like -->
3   <html>
4    <!-- the title will appear on the page-->
5   <head>
6    <title>Employee Interests Survey</title>
7   </head>
8   <body>
9    <!-- as it is a survey form, we will need to submit the details, hence we use form -->
10   <!-- We can give absolute url, or relative url like /nextpage.jsp, and specify POST or GET method -->
11  <form action="http://google.co.in">
12   <!-- If we remove this, every thing will move to the left of the page-->
13  <div align="center">
14   <!--Adds a heading to the form-->
15   <h1>Employee Interests Survey form</h1>
16   Enter your name:
17   <!-- Input type text for small texts, specify size -->
18   <input type="text" name="UserName" size=35 maxlength=35 value="">
19   <!--Adds spaces - remove and see what happens -->
20   </br></br>
21   Enter your department:
22   <input type="text" name="Deptt" size=35 maxlength=35 value=""> </br> </br>
23   Tell us a little about yourself:
24  <!-- For writing lot of text like descriptions with text wrapping,
25  if you dont want text wrapping, you can add wrap = "off" (horizontal scrollbar -->
26   <textarea name="Comments" cols=30 rows=4></textarea> </br> </br>
27   Do you exercise at home?
28   <!-- Radio buttons help you choose one out of the many values -->
29   <input type="radio" name="exe" value=1>Yes
30   <input type="radio" name="exe" value=2>No
31  </p>
32   How do you like to read about your favorite topics?
33  <p>
34   <!--Checkbox lets you select multiple options -->
35   <input type="checkbox" name="Books">Books
36   <input type="checkbox" name="Web">Online resources
37   <input type="checkbox" name="Phone">Phone apps
38   <input type="checkbox" name="Magazines">Magazines
39  </p>
40   What genre of movies do you like?
41   <!--Select box lets you choose one of the multiple dropdown options-->
42  <select name="moviepref" ><option>
43  <option value=1 selected = "true">comedy
44  <option value=2 >romance
45  <option value=3 >thriller
46  <option value=4 >horror
47  <option value=5 >biopic
48  </select>
49   </br></br>
50   <!--submits the information entered in the form by the user -->
51   <input type=submit value="Submit form">
52  </div>
53  </form>
54  </body>
55  </html>
```

OUTPUT: Here is how your page will look like:

6.1 Technical Documentation Page

Any language, piece of software, piece of machinery, and so on has professional documents for knowledge and assistance. Here's how to make the documentation page linking with internal from the navigation on the left to the information on the right. For an example of how these pages might look, look at the documentation for Python, Java, and Arduina. The majority of technological literature has many hierarchies and pages; however, we've built a basic project to get you started. You are free to extend and apply to it as you see fit. If you're just getting started with HTML, technical documentation might be a useful HTML project.

```
 1  <html>
 2  <!--This example uses the default bootstrap stylesheet-->
 3   <link rel="stylesheet" href="https://habibturi.com"
 4          integrity="sha384-BVYiiSIPeKldGmJRAkycuHAHRg32OmUcww7on3RYdg4Va+PmSTsz/K68vbdEjh4u" crossorigin="anonymous">
 5  <!--provides a full-width container that can expand or collapse based on the size of viewport-->
 6  <div class="container-fluid">
 7      <div class="row">
 8          <div class="col-md-2 col-sm-12 col-xs-12">
 9              <nav id="navbar">
10                  <h3>Technical Documentation</h3>
11                  <!--content stacking for smaller screens-->
12                  <ul class="nav nav-pills nav-stacked">
13                   <!--internal linking to the respective sections-->
14                      <a class="nav-link" href="#Introduction" rel="internal">
15                          <li>Introduction</li>
16                      </a>
17                      <a class="nav-link" href="#What_you_should_already_know" rel="internal">
18                          <li>What you should already know</li>
19                      </a>
20                      <a class="nav-link" href="#About_Topic" rel="internal">
21                          <li>About the topic</li>
22                      </a>
23                      <a class="nav-link" href="#Topic_1" rel="internal">
24                          <li>Topic 1</li>
25                      </a>
26                      <a class="nav-link" href="#Topic_2" rel="internal">
27                          <li>Topic 2</li>
28                      </a>
29                  </ul>
30              </nav>
31          </div>
32          <div class="col-md-10 col-sm-12 col-xs-12">
33              <main id="main-doc">
34                  <section class="main-section" id="Introduction" >
35                  <!--basic styling for the headings, better practice to do the same in a css file as the styling is same for all headers-->
36                      <h3 style = "background: black: color: white">Introduction</h3>
37                      <article>
38                      <p>Some content about the main topic, for example Java documentation introduction about the language
39                          </article>
```

```
40              </section>
41              <section class="main-section" id="What_you_should_already_know">
42                  <h3 style = "background: black; color: white">What you should already know</h3>
43                  <article>
44                      <p>Background information before getting into the topic:</p>
45   <!--creating list using html-->
46                          <li>Some list content</li>
47                          <li>Prerequisites.</li>
48                          <li>Workings and assumptions</li>
49                          <p>Any other content to be covered before learning this topic</p>
50                      </artice>
51              </section>
52              <section class="main-section" id="About_Topic">
53                  <h3 style = "background: black; color: white">About topic</h3>
54                  <article>
55                      <p>More lines about the topic. For example, how the basic functionality works, features etc...</p>
56                      <p>
57                      Technical documentation should be thorough and to the point
58                      </p>
59                      <p>
60                      Write about features, comparisons with other languages etc
61                      </p>
62                  </article>
63              </section>
64              <section class="main-section" id="Topic_1">
65                  <h3 style = "background: black; color: white">Topic 1</h3>
66                  <article>
67                      Getting started with the actual documentation content
68                      <code>This would come in a different color and font indicating lines of code
69                      </code>
70                  </article>
71              </section>
72              <section class="main-section" id="Topic_2">
73                  <h3 style = "background: black; color: white">Topic 2</h3>
74                  <p>
75   Another topic about the main topic, for example, if the topic is Java, this could be variables or data types in Java
76                  </p>
77              </section>
78          </main>
79      </div>
80      </div>

80      </div>
81  </div>
82  </html>
```

Technical Documentation

Introduction

Some content about the main topic, for example Java documentation introduction about the language

What you should already know

Background information before getting into the topic:

- Some list content
- Prerequisites.
- Workings and assumptions

Any other content to be covered before learning this topic

About topic

More lines about the topic. For example, how the basic functionality works, features etc...

Technical documentation should be thorough and to the point

Write about features, comparisons with other languages etc

Topic 1

Getting started with the actual documentation content This would come in a different color and font indicating lines of code

Topic 2

Another topic about the main topic, for example, if the topic is Java, this could be variables or data types in Java

6.2 Animated Website Home Page

In this project, we'll build a homepage with a logo and a few menu options. For animations, you mayeven have some fun with the keyframes tag.

Take note about how the height property is used to distinguish the navigation menu from the rest of the website. To see the difference between 85vh and 100vh, add a background picture and adjust the width to 80vh or 90vh.

```
new 1.html ❌
1    <html>
2    <head>
3     <title></title>
4     <!-- Apply any styles to html pages -->
5    <style>
6     *{
7     margin:1; padding:0.5; boxsizing:border-box;
8     }
9     header{
10    Height: 90%; height: 90vh;
11    background-color: Red;
12    background-repeat: repeat;
13    background-size: cover;
14    }
15    navigation{
16    Height: 90%; height: 20vh;
17    background: blue;
18    display: flex; left justify-content: space-between;
19    align-items: center;
20    }
21    Navigation.main_menu{
22    Height: 50%;
23    display: flex; Right-justify-content: space-around;
24    }
25    main{
26    Height: 90%; height: 75vh;
27    display: flex; Right-justify-content: center;
28    align-items: center;
29    text-align: center;
30    }
31    section h3{
32    letter-spacing: 5px; font-weight: 150;
33    }
34    section h1{
35    text-transform: lowercase;
36    }
37    section div{
38    animation:changeborder 20s infinite linear;
39    border: 7px solid red;
40    }
```

```
41    @keyframes change-border{
42    8%
43    25%
44    40%
45    }
46    </style>
47    </head>
48    <body>
49    <!--we are going to create a  menu using navigation tags-->
50    <!--We are using header for indicateing the manu -->
51    <header>
52    <nav>
53    <div class = "logo" <h2 style="color:white;">MY-LOGO</h3></div>
54    <!--We are defing the menu items-->
55    <div class = "main-menu">
56    <a href="https://google.com/ideographic/html-5">Home</a>
57    < a href="https://google.com/ ideographic/html-5">About Us</a>
58    < a href="https://google.com/ ideographic/html-5">">Contact Us</a>
59    </div>
60    </nav>
61    <!--we are  creating the main section with the help div tags-->
62    <main>
63    <section>
64    <div class = "change_text"><b>WELCOME TO X.X.X. ELECTRONICS</b></div>
65    <!--make text italic-->
66    <p><i>All your electronics needs in this place</i></p><br>
67    <!--We are now creating a button -->
68    <input type = button value = "view more">
69    </section>
70    </main>
71    </header>
72    </body>
73    </html>
```

The above code will produce the following output. The color of the box will vary.

6.3 Interactive Restaurant Website

We will build an immersive restaurant homepage in which the background picture changes while we mouse over a menu choice in this project. If you click menu navigation, for example, a menu card will appear; if you hover over house, the normal will appear. For this to function, you must assign the images names and places. jQuery is used to implement this feature. Similarly, the 'order now' icon will continue to flash. We accomplished this by employing the @keyframes functionality, which we also employed in our animated website project. The code for this is as follows:

```html
new 1.html ✖
1    <html>
2    <head>
3        <style>
4            body{
5        font-size:20px;
6                color: white;
7                background-size: cover;
8            }
9            .box{ Height: 900px;
10        float:right;
11        border:1px solid none;}
12        .box ul li{
13            Height: 120px;
14            float:left;
15            margin: 10px auto;
16            text-align: center;
17        }
18   .mainmenu
19  .mainmenu a
20  .mainmenu a:hover
21  .mainmenu img{
22  position: fixed;
23  z-index: -1;
24  top:0px; left:0px; Height:100%; height: 100vh;
25  opacity: 0.9;
26  /*object-fit:cover;*/
27  transition: all ease 0.5s;
28  }
29      .wd{
30          Height: 300px;
31          height: 539px;
32          background-color: black;
33          opacity: 0.8;
34          padding: 55px;
35      }
36      .wd h1{
37          text-align: center;
38          text-transform: uppercase;
39          font-weight: 300px;
40      }
```

```
40              }
41          .wd h4{
42              text-align: justify;
43              color:darkgray;
44              font-weight: 100px;
45          }
46          .wd h2{
47              text-align: center;
48              text-transform: uppercase;
49              font-weight: normal;
50              margin: 40px auto;
51          }
52          .opt form , input[type="button"]{
53              background-color: black;
54              color:white;
55            /* padding:10px;*/
56              margin:-14px auto;
57              padding-left: 50px;
58              padding-right: 50px;
59              text-align: center;
60              font-size: 16px;
61          }
62      form, input[type="button"] {
63          animation: glowing 300ms infinite;
64          font-weight: 500%;
65          }
66          @keyframes glowing {
67      0% {
68        background-color: red;
69      }
70      50% {
71        background-color: orange;
72      }
73      100% {
74        background-color: blue;
75      }
76    }
77      </style>
78  </head>
79  <body>
80  <body>
81  <script src="https:/google.com></script>
82  <script>
83  $(function(){
84  var image = $(".mainmenu").find('img').attr('src');
85  $(".mainmenu a").mouseover(function(){
86  var newimg = $(this).attr('data-image');
87  $(this).parent().find('img').attr("src", newimg);
88  });
89  });
90  </script>
91      <div class="box">
```

```html
    <div class="box">
<div class="mainmenu">
 <img src="food.png">
 <a data-image = "food.png" href=""> Home</a>
 <a data-image = "menucard.jpg" href=""> Menu</a>
 <a href=""> FAQ</a>
 <a href=""> Contact</a>
</div>
    </div>
    <div class="wd">
 <h1> Welcome to xxx</h1>
 <h4> <i>Order delicious food online, 100% quality, safety and taste assured.</i></h4>
 <h2> Call 999999999 for reservations</h2>
<div class="opt">
<form action="" method="post">
 <input type="button" value="ORDER NOW">
</form>
</div>
</div>
</body>
</html>
```

Conclusion

This little book has already come to a close, my friends. Although I hope that now you'll be able to take CSS "off the shelf" and begin applying it in your field, we are pleased if it simply sparks your own exploration.

- At the beginning, we were looking for a way to scale CSS that addressed the following issues:

- To make managing a broad CSS codebase over time

- To allow the removal of portions of CSS code from the codebase without impacting the remaining styles

- All innovative ideas should be able to be repeated quickly.

- Change the characteristics and values of one visual variable does not have an unintended impact on others.

- Implementing any approach should only necessitate minor tooling and process improvements.

- Deprecated features can be easily cleaned by segregating CSS into modules.

- The special naming convention eliminates unintended modifications to unrelated elements by avoiding global naming conflicts, reducing precision, and reducing specificity.

- It's easy to build out modern designs because all new modules are 'greenfield'.

- Despite some tooling to help globing imports and linting, we continue to write CSS in CSS scripts, which makes onboarding developers even simpler.

- Not just for assistive technology, but even in a broader context, we should use ARIA to monitor and convey state transition.

- CSS scaling issues are a very niche endeavor. CSS Scoping will be available in the future, but before then, we must make do with the resources and strategies we have at our disposal to bend current technologies to our will.

www.ingramcontent.com/pod-product-compliance
Lightning Source LLC
Chambersburg PA
CBHW060159060326
40690CB00018B/4176